Pressure Cooking For The Home Cook

Raya .B Snow

All rights reserved. Copyright © 2023 Raya .B Snow

COPYRIGHT © 2023 Raya .B Snow

All rights reserved.

No part of this book must be reproduced, stored in a retrieval system, or shared by any means, electronic, mechanical, photocopying, recording, or otherwise, without written permission from the publisher.

Every precaution has been taken in the preparation of this book; still the publisher and author assume no responsibility for errors or omissions. Nor do they assume any liability for damages resulting from the use of the information contained herein.

Legal Notice:

This book is copyright protected and is only meant for your individual use. You are not allowed to amend, distribute, sell, use, quote or paraphrase any of its part without the written consent of the author or publisher.

Introduction

In the world of modern cooking, the Electric Pressure Cooker stands out as a true kitchen champion, offering efficiency, convenience, and flavor-packed results like no other appliance. If you've ever wondered how this culinary powerhouse can revolutionize your home cooking, you've come to the right place.

Welcome to this book, where we embark on a journey to unlock the full potential of this remarkable kitchen gadget. Whether you're an experienced chef or a novice home cook, you're about to discover a world of flavors and possibilities that will leave you astounded.

But first, let's start with the basics. What exactly is an Electric Pressure Cooker, and why should you consider adding one to your culinary arsenal? In the opening chapters of this cookbook, we'll demystify this remarkable device and explore the compelling reasons why it has become a staple in kitchens around the globe.

Once you understand the magic behind the Electric Pressure Cooker, we'll guide you through the fundamental steps of pressure cooking. From safety tips to time-saving techniques, we'll ensure that you're well-prepared to dive into the world of pressure cooking with confidence.

Now, let's talk about the real heart of this cookbook—the recipes. Within these pages, you'll find a diverse and mouthwatering selection of dishes that cover all aspects of your culinary journey. From hearty breakfasts that will kickstart your day to delectable desserts that will satisfy your sweet tooth, we've got you covered.

If you're a fan of savory soups, tantalizing snacks, or appetizers that impress, we have recipes that will delight your taste buds. Our chicken and poultry recipes are sure to become family favorites, while our pork, beef, and lamb dishes will redefine your notion of tender, flavorful meats.

Seafood lovers will relish the fish and seafood recipes that capture the essence of the ocean, while rice and pasta enthusiasts will discover innovative ways to elevate these staple ingredients. And for those seeking plant-based options, our vegetarian recipes offer a bounty of delicious choices.

To top it all off, our dessert recipes will satisfy your cravings for something sweet, with treats that are as easy to make as they are delightful to devour.

So, whether you're looking to whip up a quick weeknight meal or impress your guests with a gourmet feast, this book is your trusted companion. Get ready to explore a world of culinary possibilities, unlock the full potential of your Electric Pressure Cooker, and savor every moment of your cooking journey. Let's get started!

Contents

Overview 1
    What is an Electric Pressure Cooker? 1
    Why Use an electric pressure cooker? 2
    Basic Steps for Pressure Cooking 4
    Some Tips for Using an Electric Pressure Cooker 4

Breakfast Recipes 12
    Breakfast Bread Pudding 12
    4-Minute Applesauce! 14
    Pressure Cooker Yogurt 15
    Steel Cut Oats 17
    Perfect Boiled Eggs 18
    Breakfast Quinoa 19

Soup Recipes 20
    Black Bean Soup 20
    Butternut Squash Soup 22
    Clam Chowder 23
    Hearty Potato Soup 25
    Minestrone 26

Snack & Appetizer Recipes 28
    Festive 7-Layer Dip 28
    Asparagus Wrapped in Prosciutto 31
    French Dip Sandwiches 32
    Homemade Ricotta Cheese 33
    Chocolate Chip Pumpkin Bread 34

- Chicken & Poultry Recipes 36
  - Braised Turkey Wings 36
  - Lemon Garlic Chicken 38
  - Salsa Verde Chicken 40
  - Moroccan Sticky Chicken 41
  - Quick Roasted Chicken 43
- Pork Recipes 45
  - BBQ Ribs 45
  - Carnitas 47
  - Chinese Pork Belly 49
  - Kahlua Pork 50
  - Quick Pork Chops 51
- Beef Recipes 53
  - Beef Stew 53
  - Braised Beef 55
  - Korean Beef 57
  - Smoked Brisket 58
  - Pot Roast 60
- Lamb Recipes 62
  - Lamb Curry 62
  - Lamb Stew 64
- Fish & Seafood Recipes 65
  - Lemon Salmon 65
  - Southern Shrimp Boil 66
  - Fish Curry 67
  - Mussels with Radicchio 69
- Rice & Pasta Recipes 71

- Lasagna 71
- Mexican Green Rice 74
- Risotto with Zucchini 75
- Spaghetti with Meatballs 77

Vegetarian Recipes 80
- Mashed Potatoes 80
- Refried Beans 82
- Sicilian Vegetable Medley 83
- Steamed Artichoke Blooms 85
- Brussels Sprouts with Sweet Orange Sauce 87

Dessert Recipes 88
- Baked Apples 88
- Cheese Flan 89
- Crème Brulée 91
- Key Lime Pie 93

Overview

There is a new gadget that gives us fast, healthy food! This amazing technology affords us convenience, speed, flavor, *and* nutrition in preparing food at home. Indeed, this kitchen device perfectly suits our modern pace of life – fast and easy food that is also wholesome and delicious.

The Electric pressure cooker is being hailed by some as nothing short of a modern-day miracle in the kitchen. This state-of-the-art electric pressure cooker is a godsend, especially to those familiar with the cumbersome and even dangerous stovetop pressure cookers of the past.

What is an Electric Pressure Cooker?

It's a **safe and easy-to-use version** of the old fashioned, stove top pressure cooker. This contraption has come a long way since back in your mother's or grandmother's day! **It can now do multiple things like sauté, pressure cooking, slow cooking, etc., making it a real multi-cooker**. It truly becomes your unique go-to kitchen tool. There are a multitude of well-known brands on the market like Cuisinart, Instant Pot, Fagor, Fissler, Gourmia, Go Wise, Harvest Cookware, Kuhn Rikon, Magefesa, Media, and Power Pressure Cooker. Sizes vary from four to eight quarts, and inserts may be stainless steel or non-stick.

The electric pressure cooker that are now available serve multi purposes including rice cooker, sauté pan, slow cooker, steamer, warmer, and even a yogurt maker. It udually has pre-programmed settings for cooking beans, chili, poultry, rice, soup, and stews. You can just press the appropriate button and leave the electric pressure cooker to do the rest.

Basically, operating an electric pressure cooker simply involves placing the ingredients in the pot, closing the lid, and choosing the right function or manually setting the timer. The electric pressure cooker will adjust its pressure and maintain it. At the end of the cooking time, it will bring down the pressure on its own and then keep the food warm.

Why Use an electric pressure cooker?

Professional chefs and ordinary home cooks alike absolutely love the electric pressure cooker for a number of reasons. Check out some of the benefits:

1. It's fast – Because pressure builds up in the pot, foods reach a higher temperature and are cooked in a much shorter time. Imagine a whole chicken done in only 25 minutes, or a large slab of pork cooked and tender in just 15 minutes!
2. It's safe – You no longer have to watch and regulate the heat during the cooking process, because an electric pressure cooker regulates itself. It also works more quietly, so there's no distressing hissing, rattling, or explosive noises. Electric pressure cooker has safety mechanisms and will not open unless it is completely depressurized.
3. It's easy to use – Some call it "set and forget." After you've set the timer, you can rely on the electric pressure cooker to do the rest. No need to check it or constantly make adjustments. The pre-programmed functions have been

tested and ensure that you get successful results. Also, because of its power, you'll have no problems cooking meals in large quantities.
4. It's space saving - You can do away with your rice cooker, sauté pan, and slow cooker. In fact, it may be all you'll need on your kitchen counter. It's ideal to use if you don't have much space in your kitchen.
5. It's versatile – As you can see in this cookbook, there are a variety of dishes that you can make – from boiled eggs to stews and even desserts.
6. It's easy to clean – In addition to being dishwasher safe, the stainless steel insert is easy to scrub clean. Because it has a sauté function, you will not need to wash any extra pans or skillets.
7. It's energy-efficient – Food is cooked in a shorter time because moisture and heat are locked in. You can cook in bulk and freeze portions to be reheated throughout the week.
8. It preserves nutrients – Because the cooking time is shortened, more nutrients are preserved. In fact, according to 1995 research, pressure cooking preserves as much as 95% of nutrients and this is more than any other cooking method (boiling preserve on average 40% of nutrient. Roasting and steaming preserve anywhere from 50% to 90% of the nutrient
9. It gives tastier results – Flavors are locked in and retained during cooking. The soft morsels of food readily coat the tongue, enhancing flavor perception.
10. It enhances digestion – Phytic acid and lectin, substances in beans and grains that interfere with digestion and absorption of nutrients, are greatly reduced by pressure cooking.

Basic Steps for Pressure Cooking

Using an electric pressure cooker as a pressure cooker involves these basic steps:

1. Know what your cooking time should be – Initially, it is best to follow the recipes or the instruction manual from the manufacturer. Eventually, you will be able to figure out how to manipulate the cooking time to get the results you want.
2. Make sure your pressure cooker is clean – Check for any debris that could interfere with its performance.
3. Place ingredients in the pot – If you've decided how long your cooking time should be, and all parts of the pot are spic and span, you're now ready to fill the insert or inner pot.
4. Place the lid – Turn it clockwise to lock.
5. Plug it in – Now that it's filled and locked, you can go ahead and plug it in. A beep will signal that your electric pressure cooker is all set to cook.
6. Press the right buttons – Finally, you can start pressure cooking by simply pressing on the appropriate function key or by setting the time manually.

Some Tips for Using an Electric Pressure Cooker

As with every gadget, always start off by reading the user's manual carefully. Each brand and model has its own quirks, so it's best to get to know your own unit well. Understanding how your very own electric pressure cooker works will make it easy for you to adjust recipes that are made for other pressure cooker brands or cooking methods. Here are some other tips to help you get the best out of your electric pressure cooker.

Altitude
People who live 3,000 feet above sea level will have to add 5% more to the cooking time given in a recipe. Increase by another 5% for every additional 1,000 feet in altitude.

Capacity
The declared capacity of the electric pressure cooker is that for use in non-pressurized mode. For pressure cooking, you can only put in half (for beans, rice, fruit, and dehydrated food) to two-thirds (for other types of food) of the total capacity. This means that, FOR PRESSURE COOKING, a 4-quart pot can only hold 2 to 2 ⅔ quarts. You'll need a 6-quart pot to cook 4 quarts. **NEVER OVERFILL.** This could block the pressure release valve!

Clean up!
Always wash the anti-block shield, insert, and sealing ring after use. Ingredients like dairy tend to stick to the pot. Make sure there are no bits stuck to the sealing ring. These bits can impart unwanted odors and flavors, or affect cooking efficiency. When the float valve is clean, it moves easily up and down. Don't forget to keep the steam release handle clean as well, and keep it pointed toward the sealing position.

Cooking Time
There are many factors that can affect the outcome of your dish, such as the quantity, size, texture, temperature (whether frozen, chilled, or room temperature), amount of liquid, etc. It's best to start with recommended cooking times and, later, a little trial and error will sometimes help you achieve the results you want. You'll find recommended cooking times for common ingredients in the manual. Start with what's listed or given in the recipe. You can adjust the cooking time later to suit your liking.

Compared to stove top pressure cookers that operate at a pressure of 15 psi, the electric pressure cooker operates at a lower pressure of 10.15 to 11.6 psi. Add 5-10 minutes to cooking time when following a recipe for stove top pressure cookers. If you want to be more precise, compute for 7-15% of the cooking time for a stove top pressure cooker and add that to your cooking time using an electric pressure cooker.

Add 5-10 more minutes of cooking if you start with frozen food to allow for thawing. Also, remember that size determines cooking time, rather than quantity. It will take longer to bring large chunks of meat to a nice texture than it would bite-sized pieces.

Depressurizing
You can depressurize your pot two ways.

1. Natural Release – the pressure will go down by itself in 10-20 minutes.
2. Quick Release – by turning the release handle to venting position, you can release the steam immediately. Just keep away from the hot steam and do not use with the congee setting.

Durability
The electric pressure cookers of good quality are usually made of high grade, rust resistant stainless steel, so you know it will last a long time. For brands that have a non-stick insert, be careful not to scratch the surface.

Extra Insert
Buy an extra insert so you don't have to wash yours after each use. It's also very convenient to use the insert to store pressure-cooked food in the fridge, while having at least one extra for cooking more dishes.

Foaming
Some cereals and grains, especially oats, can foam while cooking, leaving bits on the lid and seal. This can be avoided by:

1. using the pot-in-pot, or PIP method (see below),
2. filling only up to the half level line,
3. adding some oil to the ingredients, or
4. allowing the pressure to go down naturally (natural release).

Flour and Starch
These ingredients tend to stick to the bottom of the pot, valves, and seals, which makes cooking and heat dissipation inefficient. It is recommended that thickeners be added at the end of the cooking process, using the warming or sauté mode.

Foil Sling
Dishes that involve the pot-in-pot method may be difficult to lift out of the cooker's pot. Make a sturdy 18-inch strip of foil, folded lengthwise twice, to make a "sling." Place the pan or bowl on the center of the foil strip and grasp the two ends. This sling makes it easy to lower and lift the pan into and out of the cooker's pot.

Frozen food
Another wonderful feature of electric pressure cookers is that you can you start cooking even while the food is still frozen. Thawing can be incorporated into the whole cooking process. When following recipes calling for non-frozen ingredients, you'll need to add a few more minutes to the cooking time.

Great tip! Food that has been frozen in round molds to fit the electric pressure cooker can be conveniently dropped in for cooking or reheating.

Liquids
One basic and perhaps the most important tip is that **you must have at least one cup of liquid** in the cooker's pot for pressure cooking, to attain desirable pressure. How much you add will depend on the moisture content of the food you're cooking. Electric pressure cookers are sealed, so very little moisture is lost while cooking. If you're not sure how the food will turn out after pressure cooking, begin with the general recommendation of 1 ½ cups of liquid to prevent the food from burning. Also, after cooking, don't throw out the liquid. It's rich in nutrients and you can use it to make broths, sauces, or gravy.

Maximum Capacity Line
Exceeding this line will make cooking inefficient and give unsatisfactory results – or worse, block the pressure release valve. Again, remember that for pressure cooking, fill only halfway (for beans, rice, fruit and dehydrated food) or two-thirds full (for other types of food).

Pot- in-Pot (PIP) Method
Set up the electric pressure cooker like a steamer by putting the trivet in the pot, filling with about an inch of water, and placing a small heatproof bowl on top. The food to be cooked is placed in the bowl and covered (you can use aluminum foil). This is especially useful when cooking thick and creamy sauces containing milk and cheese. By using the PIP Method, the water serves as the pressure seal and prevents the thick sauces from sticking to parts of the pot and interfering with cooking efficiency.

Pre-programmed Functions
With these functions at your fingertips, you don't have to guess cooking times for common ingredients. This will save you time and trouble.

Pressure/Steam Release
There are two methods: quick release and natural release. The quick release is critical when you don't want to overcook your food. Simply move the steam release handle to one side to vent. Remember that hot steam will come out at high speed, so use an oven mitt or towel for protection when releasing steam. The pressure indicator retracts so you know that it's safe to open the electric pressure cooker.

Silicone Sealing Ring
Keep a spare just in case. This needs to be changed every 18-24 months.

Be prepared for inconsistencies in cooking times. As you go along, you will learn to make adjustments and master your electric pressure cooker. The directions in the recipes are designed to make them easy to follow. This cookbook is not intended to replace your manual, but rather to help you discover and sample the array of dishes you can make using your new electric pressure cooker. Although pressure cooking definitely speeds up cooking time in general, remember that it has other benefits as well, such as better nutritive value and enhanced flavor.

An Additional Note Before You Start
Some electric pressure cookers have pressure strength options. Unless otherwise indicated, the vent should always be set to SEALING and the pressure strength setting is understood to be HIGH.

Cooking times indicated in recipes do not include the amount of time that the electric pressure cooker needs to reach the desired pressure and temperature, or the time it takes to depressurize. In general, pressure cookers will take 8-10 minutes before actual pressure cooking starts. Also, after cooking, it will take about 20 minutes for the pressure in the pot to go down naturally.

In this cookbook, you'll find an assortment of recipes for newbies and seasoned chefs alike. It's time to try it out, and find out why the Electric pressure cooker is such a hit!

Breakfast Recipes

Breakfast Bread Pudding

Serves 4-6
Preparation time: 10 minutes plus 20 minutes absorption time
Cooking time: 20 minutes

Ingredients

7 slices cinnamon bread, toasted and cubed
½ cup raisins
¼ cup crushed nuts of choice (almonds, peanuts, pecans, and walnuts are all good)
4 tablespoons butter, melted
½ cup packed brown sugar
3 cups whole milk
3 eggs, beaten
1 teaspoon vanilla
½ teaspoon cinnamon
¼ teaspoon salt
Maple syrup, honey or applesauce (optional)

Directions

1. Place the bread, raisins, and nuts in a heatproof metal or glass pan that will fit into the cooker's pot.
2. In a bowl, whisk the butter, brown sugar, milk, eggs, vanilla, cinnamon, and salt together.
3. Pour the liquid into the bread mixture, and stir.
4. Let it sit for 20 minutes, stirring occasionally.
5. Cover the bowl with foil.
6. Fill the cooker's pot with 1 ½ cups of water and place the trivet in the pot. Use a foil sling to lower the pan into the cooker's pot.

7. Cover and lock the lid, and set the timer to 20 minutes.
8. Quick release, and wait for the valve to drop.
9. Open and lift the pan out.
10. Drizzle with maple syrup, honey, or applesauce, if desired.

Nutrition (per serving)
Calories 306, carbs 46 g, fat 10 g, protein 11 g, sodium 472 mg

4-Minute Applesauce!

Serves 10
Preparation time: 5 minutes plus 25 minutes in water bath
Cooking time: 4 minutes

Ingredients

Apples, washed, cored, unpeeled (or peeled, if preferred)
1 cup sugar
1 teaspoon cinnamon or pumpkin spice
Dash of ground nutmeg (optional)
Dash of ground ginger (optional)

Directions

1. Line the electric pressure cooker insert with enough apples to fill it up to a little below the line.
2. Close and set it to steam, 4 minutes.
3. Use natural pressure release (do not quick release!)
4. Use an immersion blender to purée the apples.
5. Stir in the sugar (adjusting if needed) and the spices. Mix well.
6. Transfer the applesauce to prepared glass jars with lids.
7. Leave in a water bath for 25 minutes.
8. Serve with bread, pancakes, ice cream, bread pudding, or waffles.

Nutrition (per serving)

Calories 194, carbs 51 g. fat 1 g, protein 1 g, sodium 8 mg

Pressure Cooker Yogurt

Serves 8-12
Preparation time: 10 minutes
Cooking time: 8 hours

Ingredients
1 gallon 2% milk
¼ cup yogurt with live culture (starter)
½ cup sugar or sweetener of choice (optional)

Directions

1. Pour the milk into the pot.
2. Cover and lock the lid. Plug in the cooker.
3. Set to the pot to the yogurt setting, and adjust the display to boil.
4. Allow the boil cycle to finish (about 1 hour).
5. Set the pot to sauté and, using a thermometer, warm the mixture to 185°F.
6. Unplug the cooker, and place it on a cooling rack.
7. Allow the milk to cool down to 110°F.
8. Stir in the starter and sugar, mixing well.
9. Plug in the pot again and set it to yogurt.
10. Allow the yogurt to incubate (8 hours).
11. After incubation, transfer the yogurt to a bowl and chill for 6 hours to overnight.
12. To strain, pour into a nut milk bag over a bowl. Hang up the nut milk bag, with the bowl underneath to catch the whey. Strain for ½ to 1 hour, depending on the desired thickness. Set aside the whey for other recipes. (This can be used as a buttermilk substitute.)
13. Place the yogurt in a bowl and stir, then transfer to sterilized jars for storage.

14. Refrigerate overnight before serving.

Nutrition (per serving)
Calories 149, carbs 11 g, fat 8 g, protein 9 g, sodium 113 mg

Steel Cut Oats

Serves 3-4
Preparation time: 5 minutes
Cooking time: 10 minutes

Ingredients
1 tablespoon butter
1 cup steel cut oats
1 ¾ cups water
1 cup milk
Salt
Fruits and sweetener such as honey, maple syrup for serving

Directions

1. Place the butter in the cooker's pot insert and set the pot to sauté, to melt it.
2. Add the oats and stir until toasted and fragrant (about 3 minutes).
3. Pour in the water and milk, plus the salt to taste.
4. Close the lid and lock it. Set the timer to 5 minutes.
5. After cooking, use the natural pressure release until the pressure indicator drops.
6. Open, and stir the oats.
7. Cover again, and let the pot sit until the oats have the desired consistency (about 5 minutes).
8. Serve with fruits, and sweeten to taste.

Nutrition (per serving)
Calories 150, carbs 27 g, fat 2 g, protein 5 g, sodium 230 mg

Perfect Boiled Eggs

Serves 4
Preparation time: 5 minutes
Cooking time: 12 minutes

Ingredients
4 eggs (or more)

Directions

1. Place the trivet in the cooker's pot and add 1 cup water.
2. Place the eggs on the trivet.
3. Set the timer to 6 minutes.
4. Use the natural release for 6 minutes, and then quick release.
5. Immediately transfer the eggs to an ice bath. Soak for 5-7 minutes.
6. Peel and serve.

Nutrition (per serving)
Calories 77, carbs 1 g, fat 5 g, protein 6 g, sodium 62 mg

Breakfast Quinoa

Serves 6
Preparation time: 5 minutes
Cooking time: 11 minutes

Ingredients

1 ½ cups uncooked quinoa, well rinsed
2 ¼ cups water
2 tablespoons maple syrup
½ teaspoon vanilla
¼ teaspoon ground cinnamon
Salt
Milk or cream, for serving
Nuts and/or fruit, for serving

Directions

1. Mix the quinoa, water, maple syrup, vanilla, cinnamon, and salt together in the cooker's pot.
2. Close the lid, and set the timer to 1 minute.
3. Natural release for 10 minutes and then quick release.
4. Wait for the valve to drop before opening the pot.
5. Fluff the quinoa with a fork.
6. Serve with milk or cream, and nuts or fruit.

Nutrition (per serving)

Calories 189, carbs 36 g, fat 3 g, protein 6 g, sodium 51 mg

Soup Recipes

Black Bean Soup

Serves 8
Preparation time: 10 minutes
Cooking time: 30 minutes

Ingredients
1 tablespoon olive oil
1 large onion, chopped
3 stalks celery, chopped
3 large carrots, chopped
1 teaspoon paprika
½ teaspoon ground cumin
½ teaspoon salt
¼ teaspoon pepper
2 cloves garlic, minced
2 cups ham, chopped
1 (15 ounce) can tomato sauce
8 cups chicken stock
2 cups dried black beans, cleaned and rinsed
Salt and pepper, to taste

Directions

1. Set the electric pressure cooker to sauté.
2. When the cooker's pot is ready, add the olive oil.
3. Sauté the onions with the celery, carrots, and spices, until the edges begin to brown (about 5 minutes).
4. Add the garlic and cook until fragrant (about 30 seconds).
5. Add the ham, tomato sauce, stock, and beans. Cover and lock, making sure the steam nozzle is sealed.
6. Set the timer to 25 minutes.

7. Natural release for 15 minutes. If the pressure indicator has not retracted after 15 minutes, quick release.
8. Adjust the taste with salt and pepper as desired, and serve warm.

Nutrition (per serving)
Calories 225 g, carbs 19 g, fat 10 g, protein 17 g, sodium 514 mg

Butternut Squash Soup

Serves 3-4
Preparation time: 5 minutes
Cooking time: 20 minutes

Ingredients
1 tablespoon olive oil
1 large onion, chopped
4 pounds butternut squash, peeled, seeded, and cubed, divided
1 sprig sage
1 thumb ginger, peeled and sliced
¼ teaspoon nutmeg
4 cups chicken or vegetable stock
1-2 tablespoons butter
2 tablespoons sour cream (optional)
Salt and pepper to taste

Directions

1. Set the cooker's pot to sauté.
2. Add the olive oil and sauté the onions with 1 cup of the cubed squash until slightly browned (about 10 minutes).
3. Stir in the sage, ginger, nutmeg, and stock.
4. Add the remaining squash. Cover and lock, making sure the steam nozzle is sealed.
5. Set the timer to 15 minutes.
6. Quick release, and remove the sage stem.
7. Stir in the butter, and season with salt and pepper.
8. Use an immersion blender to purée the mixture.
9. Adjust the taste with more salt and pepper, if needed.
10. Drizzle with sour cream (optional) and serve.

Nutrition (per serving)
Calories 90 g, carbs 18 g, fat 2 g, protein 2 g, sodium 485 mg

Clam Chowder

Serves 3-4
Preparation time: 5 minutes
Cooking time: 15 minutes

Ingredients
½-1 tablespoon olive oil (optional)
1 cup bacon, cubed
1 medium onion, finely chopped
Black pepper, to taste
½ cup white wine
2 cups clam juice (or fish or vegetable stock)
2 medium potatoes, unpeeled, cubed
1 bay leaf
1 sprig thyme
1 pinch cayenne or paprika
11 ounces clams (fresh, frozen or canned), washed and drained
1 cup milk
1 cup cream

For roux
1 tablespoon flour
1 tablespoon butter

Directions

1. Set the electric pressure cooker to sauté.
2. Add a little olive oil (if using), and the bacon. Bring to a sizzle.
3. Add the onion and sprinkle with pepper. Continue sautéing until the onion is tender (about 5 minutes).
4. Deglaze with wine, scraping any bits from the bottom. Continue stirring until the mixture is almost dry.

5. Add the clam juice or stock, potatoes, bay leaf, thyme, and cayenne. Cover and lock, making sure the steam nozzle is sealed.
6. Set the timer to 5 minutes.
7. While the potatoes are cooking, prepare the roux by mixing the flour and butter together in a pan over medium-low heat. Blend well (about 3 minutes).
8. When 5 minutes are up, quick release the pressure.
9. Stir in the clams, milk, cream, and roux. Set to sauté, if needed. Continue stirring until the mixture begins to thicken (about 5 minutes).
10. Serve with bread or crackers.

Nutrition (per serving)
Calories 162, carbs 19 g, fat 6 g, protein 9 g, sodium 1144 mg

Hearty Potato Soup

Serves 4
Preparation time: 5 minutes
Cooking time: 12 minutes

Ingredients
5 cups potato, peeled and diced
1 large onion, chopped
10 cloves garlic, minced
1 tablespoon salt
8 cups chicken stock
1 cup cream cheese

For garnish
¼ cup cheddar cheese, grated
¼ cup cooked bacon pieces

Directions

1. Place the potato, onion, garlic, salt, and chicken stock in the cooker's pot.
2. Cover and lock, making sure the steam nozzle is sealed.
3. Set the pot to the soup or manual setting, for 10 minutes.
4. Quick release, cancel, and change to the sauté setting.
5. Stir in the cream cheese until the soup is well blended (about 2 minutes).
6. Serve garnished with grated cheese and bacon.

Nutrition (per serving)
Calories 136, carbs 17 g, fat 5 g, protein 6 g, sodium 1052 mg

Minestrone

Serves 8
Preparation time: 10 minutes
Cooking time: 16 minutes

Ingredients
2 tablespoons olive oil
2 stalks celery, diced
1 large onion, diced
1 large carrot, diced
3 cloves garlic, minced
1 teaspoon oregano
1 teaspoon basil
Salt and pepper, to taste
1 (28 ounce) can tomatoes, puréed
4 cups chicken broth
1 bay leaf
½ cup fresh spinach, shredded
1 cup small pasta of choice
⅓ cup grated Parmesan cheese
1 (15 ounce) can white kidney beans, drained

Directions

1. Set the pot to sauté.
2. When it is ready, add the olive oil, celery, onion, carrot, and garlic. Sauté until the vegetables are tender (about 5 minutes).
3. Stir in the rest of the ingredients EXCEPT the white kidney beans.
4. Cover and lock, making sure the steam nozzle is sealed.
5. Set the timer to 6 minutes.
6. When 6 minutes is up, wait 2 minutes, then quick release.

7. Add the kidney beans, stir, and allow them to heat through (about 3 minutes).
8. Garnish with more Parmesan, if desired.

Nutrition (per serving)
Calories 160, carbs 26 g, fat 4 g, protein 7 g, sodium 560 mg

Snack & Appetizer Recipes

Festive 7-Layer Dip

Serves 15-20
Preparation time: 30 minutes
Cooking time: 0 minutes

Ingredients

For the refried beans layer
1 recipe refried beans

For the cheese layer
1 cup cheddar cheese, grated

For the guacamole layer
1 large avocado, mashed
1 garlic clove, crushed and minced
1 teaspoon lime juice
1 pinch salt

For the cream layer
1 cup plain yogurt or sour cream

For the salsa layer
1 large tomato, diced small and strained
2 tablespoons onion, finely chopped
3 sprigs cilantro (or parsley), finely chopped

Remaining Layers
¼ cup black olives, sliced
1 green onion, finely sliced

Directions

1. Prepare the refried beans and keep them warm.

For the guacamole

2. In a bowl, combine the ingredients and set them aside.

For the salsa

3. Combine the ingredients in a bowl and mix well.
4. Place the salsa in a strainer to drain any excess liquid.
5. Set it aside.

For the cream layer

6. Drain any watery liquid layer from the yogurt or sour cream. Set it aside.

To assemble the dip

7. Layer the dip in a transparent bowl, or in individual glasses:

- Start with refried beans at bottom of the bowl or glass. Spread them evenly.
- Scoop some cheese on top of the refried beans, starting from the center and spreading it outward as evenly as possible to the sides.
- Follow with guacamole, and spread it the same way.

- Spread the yogurt or cream over the guacamole, covering the edges to seal the layer and prevent the guacamole from turning brown.
- Follow the cream layer with the salsa. It should be well drained to prevent the dip from becoming diluted by liquid or moisture from the tomatoes.
- Arrange the olives over the salsa layer.
- Finally, sprinkle with green onion.

8. Serve with tortilla chips or cut vegetables.

Nutrition (per serving)
Calories 114, carbs 8 g, fat 6 g, protein 6 g, sodium 253 mg

Asparagus Wrapped in Prosciutto

Serves 2-3
Preparation time: 5 minutes
Cooking time: 7 minutes

Ingredients
1 pound thick asparagus
8 ounces thinly sliced Prosciutto

Directions

1. Fill the cooker's pot with 1-2 cups water, following the minimum amount as stated in the manual.
2. Wrap the asparagus spears individually with Prosciutto.
3. Lay any extra asparagus in a single layer on the bottom of the steamer basket. (If there is no excess, oil the steamer basket to prevent the wrapped asparagus from sticking.)
4. Lay the wrapped asparagus in the basket.
5. Lower the steamer basket into the cooker's pot.
6. Set the timer to 2 minutes.
7. Use natural release, and open the pot.
8. Immediately remove the steamer basket to prevent overcooking.

Nutrition (per serving)
Calories 81, carbs 2 g, fat 4 g, protein 9 g, sodium 521 mg

French Dip Sandwiches

Serves 8
Preparation time: 5 minutes
Cooking time: 35 minutes

Ingredients
4 pounds beef roast, sliced and trimmed
¾ cup soy sauce
8 buns

For the sauce
1 teaspoon beef bouillon
2 teaspoons black peppercorns
1 tablespoon rosemary, dried
2-3 cloves garlic, minced

Directions

1. Place the meat in the cooker's pot.
2. Mix the sauce ingredients and pour it over the meat.
3. Add enough water to just cover the meat.
4. Cover and lock the lid, making sure the valve is sealed.
5. Set the timer to 35 minutes.
6. Release the pressure using the quick release method.
7. Shred the meat and use as filling for the buns.

Nutrition (per serving)
Calories 492, carbs 38 g, fat 10 g, protein 59 g, sodium 1940 mg

Homemade Ricotta Cheese

Yields 2 cups
Preparation time: 5 minutes
Cooking time: 60 minutes

Ingredients
½ gallon whole milk
1 ½ teaspoons salt
⅓ cup lemon juice

Directions

1. Pour the milk into the electric pressure pot and stir in the salt.
2. Cover and lock, making sure the valve is sealed.
3. Set to yogurt, and adjust to boil.
4. As soon as the pot beeps, unplug the electric pressure cooker.
5. Open the lid and gently stir in the lemon juice.
6. Let it sit for 10 minutes to allow the milk to curdle. Do not stir.
7. Line a colander with 2 layers of cheesecloth to strain the cheese. A nut milk bag or yogurt strainer can also be used.
8. Let it drain until the desired thickness is attained (10-60 minutes).
9. Store in an airtight container. Keeps for a week, refrigerated.

Nutrition (per cup)
Calories 428 g, carbs 7 g, fat 32 g, protein 28 g, sodium 207 mg

Chocolate Chip Pumpkin Bread

Serves 6-8
Preparation time: 15 minutes
Cooking time: 50 minutes

Ingredients
1 cup rice flour
¾ cup almond flour
½ cup tapioca flour
1 teaspoon baking soda
2 large eggs
½ cup sugar
½ cup maple syrup
½ cup coconut oil
2 tablespoons pumpkin spice
1 teaspoon vanilla
1 pinch salt
½ cup chocolate chips

Directions

1. In a medium bowl, combine the rice, almond, and tapioca flours with the baking soda. Set the bowl aside.
2. In a separate bowl, whip together the rest of the ingredients EXCEPT the chocolate chips.
3. Add the dry ingredients gradually to the wet, mixing until well blended.
4. Lastly, lightly mix in the chocolate chips.
5. Grease a pan or bowl that will fit in the cooker's pot.
6. Place the trivet into the pot and add a cup of water.
7. Pour the batter into the greased pan, spreading it evenly.
8. Using a foil sling, lower the pan into the cooker's pot.
9. Close the lid, and set the timer to 50 minutes.

10. After cooking, natural release, for about 10 minutes.
11. Quick release the rest of the pressure, and lift the pan out.
12. Let the cake cool on a rack for 10 minutes.
13. Loosen the sides of the cake with a knife, and carefully flip it over to remove it from the pan.

Nutrition (per serving)
Calories 479, carbs 63 g, fat 25 g, protein 5 g, sodium 216 mg

Chicken & Poultry Recipes

Braised Turkey Wings

Serves 3
Preparation time: 5 minutes
Cooking time: 20 minutes

Ingredients
1 teaspoon thyme
½ teaspoon paprika
½ teaspoon Cajun seasoning
1 teaspoon garlic powder
½ teaspoon salt
½ teaspoon black pepper
1 teaspoon oregano
2 pounds turkey wings, tips cut off
2 tablespoons oil
1 medium onion, chopped
½ cup cooking wine
1 ½ cups chicken stock
1 ½ tablespoons Worcestershire sauce

Directions

1. Combine the thyme, paprika, Cajun seasoning, garlic powder, salt, pepper, and oregano. Rub the seasonings evenly on the wings.
2. Set the electric pressure cooker to sauté, and allow it to heat up.
3. Pour the oil into the pot, and sauté the onion until tender (about 2 minutes).
4. Add the wings and brown them evenly (about 5 minutes).
5. Add the wine, stock, and Worcestershire sauce.

6. Bring the broth to a boil and place the lid on.
7. Manually set the timer to 15 minutes.
8. After 15 minutes, do a quick release.
9. The turkey will be done, but the tenderness will depend on your preference. If you want the wings to be more tender, cook for another 5 minutes

Nutrition (per serving)
Calories 430, carbs 7 g, fat 15 g, protein 63 g, sodium 1495 mg

Lemon Garlic Chicken

Serves 4
Preparation time: 10 minutes
Cooking time: 20 minutes

Ingredients
1 tablespoon olive oil
1 onion, diced
5 cloves garlic, minced
2 pounds chicken breasts or thighs
½ cup chicken broth
¼ cup white cooking wine
Juice of 1 small lemon
1 teaspoon salt
1 teaspoon dried parsley
¼ teaspoon paprika
1 tablespoons flour

Directions

1. Set the pot to sauté until it is hot.
2. Pour in the oil, and sauté the onion until tender (about 3 minutes).
3. Add the garlic and stir until fragrant (about 1 minute).
4. Add the chicken and sear it slightly.
5. Pour in the broth, wine, and lemon juice.
6. Add the salt, parsley, and paprika.
7. Cover and lock the lid, and set it to poultry or 15 minutes.
8. Quick release, and open the lid.
9. Take a cup of the broth out of the pot for the slurry and allow it to cool slightly. Add the flour to the cup of broth and stir.

10. Pour the slurry back into the pot and stir to combine.
11. Set the pot to sauté, and cook until the sauce thickens.
12. Serve with rice.

Nutrition (per serving)
Calories 399, carbs 8 g, fat 11 g, protein 50 g, sodium 717 mg

Salsa Verde Chicken

Serves 4
Preparation time: 5 minutes
Cooking time: 25 minutes

Ingredients
2 pounds boneless chicken breasts
1 teaspoon cumin
1 teaspoon smoked paprika
1 teaspoon salt
2 cups salsa verde

Directions

1. Place the ingredients in an electric pressure cooker.
2. Set it to 25 minutes.
3. When the cooking time is finished, quick release the pressure.
4. Remove the chicken and shred it with a fork.

Nutrition (per serving)
Calories 278, carbs 4 g, fat 6 g, protein 46 g, sodium 1564 mg

Moroccan Sticky Chicken

Serves 2
Preparation time: 5 minutes
Cooking time: 50 minutes

Ingredients
1 pound chicken drumsticks, rinsed and drained
2 tablespoons cooking oil

For the spice rub
¼ teaspoon packed saffron threads
1 teaspoon paprika
1 teaspoon garlic powder
1 teaspoon ground cumin
½ teaspoon ground ginger
½ teaspoon ground cinnamon
¼ teaspoon ground coriander
1 teaspoon sea salt
½ teaspoon black pepper

For the glaze
¼ cup honey
2 teaspoons blackstrap molasses
1 medium lemon, zest and juice

Directions

To make the spice rub

> 1. Crush the saffron in a mortar and pestle, and combine it with all the other spices.

For the glaze

> 2. Whisk the glaze ingredients together in a bowl. Set it aside.

Cooking

> 3. Pat the chicken dry with paper towels.
> 4. Rub the spice rub evenly over the chicken pieces.
> 5. Set the electric pressure cooker to sauté until it is hot.
> 6. Add the oil and brown the chicken evenly (about 15 minutes).
> 7. Close the lid and make sure the valve is sealed.
> 8. Set the pot to 10 minutes.
> 9. After cooking for 10 minutes, press keep warm or cancel to stop cooking and vent out the steam.
> 10. Carefully remove the chicken from the cooker's pot and transfer it to a platter. Cover with foil and set it aside.
> 11. Set the pot to sauté with the lid off.
> 12. Add the glaze mix to the pot. Bring it to a boil, and stir occasionally. Continue cooking to reduce (about 5-15 minutes). Add water if it becomes too thick.
> 13. Coat the chicken with sauce, and serve.

Nutrition (per serving)

Calories 509, carbs 36 g, fat 27 g, protein 32 g, sodium 199 mg

Quick Roasted Chicken

Serves 4-6
Preparation time: 5 minutes
Cooking time: 55 minutes

Ingredients
1 whole chicken (about 4 pounds)
1 tablespoon olive oil
½ teaspoon garlic powder
½ teaspoon paprika
1 teaspoon dried thyme
Salt and pepper, to taste

Directions

1. Set the electric pressure cooker to sauté and add the coconut oil.
2. Season the chicken with garlic powder, paprika, thyme, salt, and pepper.
3. When the oil is hot, add the chicken and sear until it is browned on both sides.
4. Season with salt and pepper.
5. Cover and lock, sealing the valve.
6. Set the pot to poultry, and adjust the pressure to HIGH for 20 minutes.
7. After the cooking time is up, use quick release.
8. Flip the chicken over and cover it again.
9. Set the pot to 15 minutes.
10. Check for doneness, and cook longer, if needed.

Nutrition (per serving)
Calories 227, carbs 0 g, fat 17 g, protein 19 g, sodium 180 mg

Pork Recipes

BBQ Ribs

Serves 6
Preparation time: 30 minutes
Cooking time: 30 minutes

Ingredients
3 pounds baby back ribs, cut into two-rib pieces
1 tablespoon olive oil
1 large onion, diced
4 cloves garlic, minced

For the rub
2 tablespoons smoked paprika
3 tablespoons brown sugar
1 tablespoon chili powder
1 teaspoon salt
½ teaspoon black pepper

For the sauce
1 ½ cups ketchup
3 tablespoons brown sugar
3 tablespoons Worcestershire sauce
1 ½ tablespoons juice of lime or lemon
1 teaspoon dry mustard
¾ teaspoons salt

Directions

1. Mix the rub ingredients together and rub the mixture evenly over the rib pieces. Set them aside.
2. Combine the sauce ingredients in a bowl and set it aside.
3. Set the electric pressure cooker to sauté.

4. When it is hot, add the oil and sauté the onions until they are tender (about 3 minutes).
5. Add the garlic and cook momentarily, until fragrant.
6. Stir in the sauce mixture.
7. Add the ribs and coat each piece evenly.
8. Arrange the ribs so they are upright, with the meaty parts facing the sides of the pan.
9. Place the lid, and seal.
10. Set the timer to 30 minutes.
11. When the cooking time is over, natural release for 15 minutes, then quick release.
12. Remove the ribs from the pot. If desired, grill them at 400°F, about 2 minutes on each side.
13. Drizzle with more sauce, and serve.

Nutrition (per serving)
Calories 330, carbs 18 g, fat 21 g, protein 18 g, sodium 840 mg

Carnitas

Serves 8-10
Preparation time: 10 minutes
Cooking time: 50 minutes

Ingredients
2 ½ pounds pork shoulder blade roast, boneless, trimmed
1 ½ teaspoons salt
1 teaspoon black pepper
2-3 tablespoons cooking oil
6 cloves garlic, slivered
¾ cup chicken broth
3 chipotle peppers in adobo sauce
2 bay leaves

For seasoning
1 ½ teaspoons cumin
½ teaspoon sazon (Mexican seasoned salt)
¼ teaspoon dry oregano
¼ teaspoon dry adobo seasoning
½ teaspoon garlic powder

Directions

1. Combine the seasoning ingredients in a bowl. Set it aside.
2. Rub the pork with salt and pepper.
3. Set the electric pressure cooker to sauté.
4. Add the oil to the pot and brown the pork evenly (about 5 minutes).
5. Transfer the browned meat to a platter, and let it cool.
6. Cut slits into the meat and insert garlic slivers into them.
7. Rub the meat evenly with the seasoning mix and place it in the electric pressure cooker.

8. Add the broth, chipotle peppers with sauce, and bay leaves.
9. Place the lid and lock it.
10. Select the meat function, or manually set the timer to 50 minutes.
11. Use natural release. When the pressure has gone, open the pot and remove the bay leaves.
12. Shred the meat with forks and moisten well with the remaining liquid in the pot.
13. Adjust the flavor as needed, with cumin, adobo seasoning, salt, or pepper.
14. Serve as filling for tacos or burritos.

Nutrition (per serving)
Calories 160, carbs 1 g, fat 7 g, protein 20 g, sodium 397 mg

Chinese Pork Belly

Serves 8
Preparation time: 5 minutes
Cooking time: 35 minutes

Ingredients

1 tablespoon cooking oil
2 pounds pork belly, cut into large pieces about 3-5 inches long
1 thumb fresh ginger, peeled and sliced
6 cloves garlic, sliced
½ cup soy sauce
2 teaspoons sugar
3 tablespoons Chinese cooking wine
4 star anise pods
1-2 teaspoons white pepper powder
1 ½ cups water

Directions

1. Set the electric pressure cooker to sauté.
2. When it is hot, add the oil and sear the pork (about 5 minutes).
3. Add the ginger and garlic and cook, stirring continuously, until fragrant (about 2 minutes).
4. Stir in the rest of the ingredients.
5. Cover and lock the lid, sealing the vent.
6. Set the timer to 30 minutes.
7. Use quick release.
8. If desired, set the pot to sauté again, and continue cooking to reduce the sauce.

Nutrition (per serving)

Calories 454, carbs 2 g, fat 45 g, protein 8 g, sodium 941 mg

Kahlua Pork

Serves 8-12
Preparation time: 10 minutes
Cooking time: 90 minutes

Ingredients
4 pounds pork shoulder
½ cup water
1 tablespoon hickory liquid smoke
2 tablespoons sea salt
2 tablespoons oil
Banana leaves (if available)

Directions

1. Preheat the electric pressure cooker by pressing the sauté button.
2. Sear the meat on both sides.
3. Remove the meat to a platter, and cover it with foil.
4. Add the water and liquid smoke to the pot, and stir.
5. Sprinkle the meat with salt, wrap it with banana leaves (optional), and return it to the pot.
6. Replace the lid and adjust the timer manually to 90 minutes.
7. When the pressure has gone down, open the pot and remove the pork.
8. Discard the banana leaves (if using). Shred the meat with forks.
9. Drizzle a little of the liquid over the pulled pork to keep it moist.

Nutrition (per serving)
Calories 243, carbs 0 g, fat 15 g, protein 26 g, sodium 515 mg

Quick Pork Chops

Serves 4
Preparation time: 5 minutes
Cooking time: 20 hours

Ingredients
2 pounds pork chops, boneless
½ teaspoon sea salt
¼ teaspoon black pepper
1 tablespoon cooking oil
2 cloves garlic, smashed
½ teaspoon ginger, peeled and minced
¼ cup water or broth
2 tablespoons Dijon mustard
¼ cup maple syrup or honey

Directions

1. Rub the pork chops with salt and pepper.
2. Set the electric pressure cooker to Sauté and wait until it's hot.
3. Heat the oil, and sauté the garlic and ginger until it is fragrant.
4. Add the pork chops and sear them on both sides (about 4-5 minutes).
5. In a small bowl, whisk together the broth, mustard, and maple syrup. Pour the sauce over the pork chops.
6. Close and lock the lid. Set the timer to 15 minutes.
7. Quick release the pressure, and serve.

Nutrition (per serving)
Calories 280, carbs 8 g, fat 14 g, protein 28 g, sodium 269 mg

Beef Recipes

Beef Stew

Serves 3-4
Preparation time: 10 minutes
Cooking time: 35 minutes

Ingredients
1 pound beef tenderloin or stew meat, cut into chunks
1 tablespoon olive oil
1 onion, chopped
3 Yukon gold potatoes, cut into chunks
1 cup carrots, cut into chunks
Salt and pepper, to taste
2 cups beef broth
1 bay leaf
1 teaspoon paprika
1 teaspoon garlic powder
1 teaspoon onion powder
1 tablespoon tomato paste
1 tablespoon Worcestershire sauce
2 tablespoons flour

Directions

1. Put the electric pressure cooker in Sauté mode.
2. When it is hot, add the oil and brown the meat (about 3 minutes).
3. Stir in the onion, potatoes, and carrots, and sprinkle them with salt and pepper.
4. Add the rest of the ingredients EXCEPT the flour.
5. Close and lock the lid.
6. Set at meat/stew, or set the timer manually to 35 minutes.

7. When the cooking is done, use natural release.
8. Open the pot, and carefully scoop out about ¼ cup of the broth. Let it cool slightly.
9. Add the flour to the broth, and stir to make a slurry.
10. Pour the slurry back into the pot, and stir until the sauce thickens.
11. Adjust the flavor with more salt and pepper, if needed.

Nutrition (per serving)
Calories 270, carbs 26 g, fat 6 g, protein 22 g, sodium 1290 mg

Braised Beef

Serves 6-8
Preparation time: 5 minutes
Cooking time: 70 minutes

Ingredients
2 tablespoons cooking oil
1 onion, sliced
2 pounds boneless chuck roast
Salt and pepper, to taste
½ cup red wine
½ cup beef broth
3 sprigs fresh rosemary
½ teaspoon garlic powder

Directions

1. Set the electric pressure cooker to sauté.
2. When it is hot, add the oil and sauté the onions until softened (about 2 minutes).
3. Place the meat in the pot and cook until brown (about 4 minutes on each side). Sprinkle with salt and pepper.
4. Add the rest of the ingredients to the pot.
5. Close and lock the lid, and set the timer to 60 minutes.
6. After the hour, allow the pot to natural release for 15 minutes, and then quick release to vent out any remaining pressure.
7. Press cancel, and open the pot.
8. Remove the meat and transfer it to a cutting board. Cut it into chunks.
9. Discard the rosemary stems.
10. Set the pot to sauté, and bring the sauce to a boil. Continue cooking until the sauce is reduced by half.

11. Place the beef in a serving dish, and pour the sauce over it.

Nutrition (per serving)
Calories 167, carbs 2 g, fat 1 g, protein 20 g, sodium 96 mg

Korean Beef

Serves 6
Preparation time: 15 minutes
Cooking time: 45 minutes

Ingredients

4 pounds bottom roast, cut into cubes
Salt and pepper
2 tablespoons cooking oil
1 cup beef broth
½ cup soy sauce
5 cloves garlic, minced
1 tablespoon ginger, grated
1 pear, peeled and chopped
Juice of 1 orange

Directions

1. Season the meat with salt and pepper.
2. Set the electric pressure cooker to sauté.
3. When the pot is hot, add the oil and meat and cook until it is evenly browned (about 8-10 minutes).
4. Transfer the meat to a plate.
5. Pour the broth into the pot and loosen any brown bits.
6. Stir in the soy sauce.
7. Return the meat to the pot, and add the rest of the ingredients.
8. Place the lid and lock it. Set the timer to 45 minutes.
9. After cooking, use quick release.
10. Shred the meat with forks.
11. Serve with rice.

Nutrition (per serving)

Calories 217, carbs 3 g, fat 11 g, protein 23 g, sodium 715 mg

Smoked Brisket

Serves 6
Preparation time: 10 minutes plus overnight marinating time
Cooking time: 60 minutes

Ingredients

3 pounds beef brisket, flat cut, fat trimmed
2 tablespoons liquid smoke
1 tablespoon Worcestershire sauce
½ cup water
1 cup barbecue sauce (store-bought or homemade)

For the rub
1 teaspoon seasoned meat tenderizer
¼ teaspoon celery salt
¼ teaspoon salt
½ teaspoon garlic powder
½ teaspoon onion powder
¼ teaspoon turmeric powder
½ teaspoon paprika
1 teaspoon sugar

Directions

1. The day before cooking, combine the ingredients for the rub.
2. Rub the seasonings evenly over the meat.
3. Place the meat in a resealable bag.
4. Add the liquid smoke and Worcestershire sauce to the bag, then seal.
5. Let the meat marinate overnight in the refrigerator.
6. When you are ready to cook, transfer the meat and marinade to the electric pressure cooker.
7. Add the water and barbecue sauce.

8. Close the lid and seal it. Set the timer to 60 minutes.
9. Allow natural release for 15 minutes, then quick release.
10. Cut the meat into chunks and serve with cooking liquid or more barbecue sauce, if desired.

Nutrition (per serving)
Calories 370, carbs 20 g, fat 9 g, protein 49 g, sodium 803 mg

Pot Roast

Serves 6
Preparation time: 5 minutes
Cooking time: 70 minutes

Ingredients

3 ½ pounds beef chuck or rump roast
Salt and pepper
1 tablespoon cooking oil
1 large onion, chopped
1 ½ cups beef broth
2 bay leaves
2 tablespoons flour

Directions

1. Rub the roast evenly with salt and pepper.
2. Set the electric pressure cooker to sauté.
3. When it is hot, add the oil and brown the meat (about 8-10 minutes).
4. Remove the meat from the pan.
5. Add the onion to the pot and cook until it is softened (about 3 minutes).
6. Put the meat back into the pot and pour in the broth. Drop in the bay leaves.
7. Cover and lock the lid. Set the timer to 70 minutes.
8. After cooking, use natural release for 10 minutes, and then quick release.
9. Transfer the meat to a serving platter, and discard the bay leaves.
10. Scoop out a small amount of the cooking liquid, and add the flour to it. Stir to make a slurry.

11. Pour the slurry into the pot and stir until the gravy thickens.
12. Slice the meat and serve with the gravy.

Nutrition (per serving)
Calories 344, carbs 2 g, fat 17 g, protein 45 g, sodium 297 mg

Lamb Recipes

Lamb Curry

Serves 6
Preparation time: 15 minutes plus 30 minutes marinating time
Cooking time: 25 minutes

Ingredients
1 ½ pounds cubed lamb stew meat or leg of lamb, cut in chunks
1 tablespoon butter or ghee (or cooking oil)
1 (14 ounce) can diced tomatoes
1 ½ tablespoons curry powder
1 medium onion, minced
3 medium carrots, cut into chunks

For the marinade
4 cloves garlic, minced
1 tablespoon ginger, grated
½ cup coconut milk
Juice of half a lime
Salt and pepper

Directions

1. Combine the ingredients for the marinade in a resealable bag. Add the meat and marinate for 30 minutes to overnight in the refrigerator.
2. After marinating, add the meat and marinade to the Cooker's pot.
3. Stir in the rest of the ingredients.
4. Close and lock the lid, and set the timer to 20 minutes.
5. Use natural release for 15 minutes, and then quick release.

6. Open the pot and set it to sauté. Let it cook to thicken the sauce (about 5 minutes).
7. Serve.

Nutrition (per serving)
Calories 230, carbs 11 g, fat 9 g, protein 25 g, sodium 432 mg

Lamb Stew

Serves 4-6
Preparation time: 10 minutes
Cooking time: 45 minutes

Ingredients
1 pound lamb shoulder, cut into large chunks
Salt and pepper
1 tablespoon flour
2-3 tablespoons olive oil
1 medium carrot, cut into chunks
1 large potato, peeled and cut into chunks
1 medium onion, minced
½ green pepper, seeded and cut into bite-sized pieces
1 ¾ cups beef stock

Directions

1. Season the lamb meat with salt and pepper, and coat it with flour.
2. Set the electric pressure cooker to sauté.
3. When the pot is hot, add the olive oil.
4. Sear the meat (about 7-10 minutes).
5. Add the onion and cook until fragrant (about 3 minutes).
6. Add the rest of the ingredients.
7. Cover, and lock the lid. Set the timer to 35 minutes.
8. When the cooking time is done, use quick release.
9. Serve.

Nutrition (per serving)
Calories 249, carbs 19 g, fat 13 g, protein 25 g, sodium 423 mg

Fish & Seafood Recipes

Lemon Salmon

Serves 4
Preparation time: 5 minutes
Cooking time: 5 minutes

Ingredients
4 pieces salmon fillet (about 1 inch thick)
Salt and pepper
⅛ teaspoon cayenne powder, or to taste
½ teaspoon lemon zest
Juice of 1 lemon

Directions

1. Season the salmon with all the other ingredients.
2. Pour 1 cup of water into the electric pressure cooker and place the trivet inside.
3. Arrange the salmon on the trivet.
4. Close and lock the lid, and set the timer to 5 minutes.
5. When the cooking time is done, quick release to prevent overcooking from residual heat.
6. Serve.

Nutrition (per serving)
Calories 270, carbs 12 g, fat 11 g, protein 36 g, sodium 960 mg

Southern Shrimp Boil

Serves 4-6
Preparation time: 5 minutes
Cooking time: 20 minutes

Ingredients
1 (16 ounce) can beer
1 tablespoon boiled shrimp seasoning (like Old Bay)
Salt and pepper, to taste
2 bay leaves
Hot sauce, to taste
2 onions, chopped
8 cloves garlic, peeled and crushed
1 pound potatoes, cut into chunks
4 ears of corn, cut into thirds
12 ounces Andouille sausage, cooked
1 ½ pounds fresh shrimp (in shells, deveined)
Green onions, chopped, for garnish

Directions

1. Put all the ingredients EXCEPT the green onions in the cooker's pot.
2. Cover, and lock the lid, and set the timer to 5 minutes.
3. Quick release the pressure, and discard the bay leaves.
4. Garnish with chopped green onion.
5. Serve with bread.

Nutrition (per serving)
Calories 336, carbs 39 g, fat 4 g, protein 31 g, sodium 874 mg

Fish Curry

Serves 2
Preparation time: 10 minutes
Cooking time: 5 minutes

Ingredients
1-2 tablespoons coconut oil
3 cloves garlic, minced
1 thumb ginger, grated
2 tablespoons curry powder
1 teaspoon turmeric
1 (13 ½ ounce) can coconut cream
2 cups chicken broth
2 carrots, peeled and chopped into chunks
3 ribs celery, roughly chopped
2 tomatoes, diced
3 bay or kaffir lime leaves
1 pound fish steak (you can use tilapia, mackerel, tuna, yellowtail kingfish, tuna or catfish), cut into chunks
Salt or fish sauce, to taste
Cilantro, roughly chopped, for garnish

Directions

1. Set the electric pressure cooker to sauté.
2. When it is hot, add the oil and sauté the garlic and ginger until fragrant (about 2 minutes).
3. Stir in the curry powder and turmeric until fragrant (about 1 minute).
4. Pour in the coconut cream and broth. Stir and scrape any bits from the bottom of pot insert.
5. Add the carrots, celery, tomatoes, and bay or kaffir leaves. Mix well.

6. Add the fish.
7. Cover and lock the lid, and set the timer to 3 minutes.
8. After cooking, do a quick release to avoid overcooking the fish.
9. Adjust the flavor with salt or fish sauce according to taste.
10. Serve garnished with cilantro.

Nutrition (per serving)
Calories 382, carbs 22 g, fat 29 g, protein 39 g, sodium 1210 mg

Mussels with Radicchio

Serves 6
Preparation time: 5 minutes
Cooking time: 5 minutes

Ingredients
2 pounds mussels, cleaned and de-bearded
1-2 tablespoons olive oil
1 onion, chopped
1 clove garlic, smashed
½ cup dry white wine
½ cup fish or chicken broth
1 small head of radicchio, cut into thin strips
1 pound baby spinach, cut into thin strips

Directions

1. Place the mussels in the steamer basket.
2. Set the electric pressure cooker to sauté.
3. Add the oil, and sauté the onion and garlic until softened (about 3 minutes).
4. Deglaze the pot with wine and broth.
5. Place the trivet in the pot and position the steamer basket with mussels on top of it.
6. Close and lock the lid.
7. Set the timer to 1 minute.
8. When the cooking time is done, do a quick release to prevent overcooking.
9. Quickly but carefully, scoop out the mussels with a slotted spoon and place them on a bed of radicchio and spinach strips.
10. Adjust the taste of the cooking liquid with salt, if needed.

11. Ladle hot cooking liquid over the mussels, and serve.

Nutrition (per serving)
Calories 299, carbs 17 g, fat 7 g, protein 37 g, sodium 573 mg

Rice & Pasta Recipes

Lasagna

Serves 6
Preparation time: 20 minutes
Cooking time: 7 minutes

Ingredients
8 ounces lasagna noodles, no-boil
2 cups mozzarella cheese, shredded, divided

For the cheese layer
4 cups ricotta
2 eggs, slightly beaten
⅓ cup Parmesan, grated
3 cloves garlic, minced
1 teaspoon Italian seasoning
Salt and pepper

For the meat layer
1 tablespoon olive oil
1 onion, diced
1 pound ground beef
Salt and pepper
1 (24 ounce) jar pasta sauce
¼ cup water

Directions

<u>To make the cheese layer</u>

1. Combine all the ingredients in a bowl. Mix well, and set aside.

<u>For the meat layer</u>

2. Set the electric pressure cooker to sauté.
3. When the pot is hot, add the oil, onion, and beef.
4. Cook, with stirring, until the onion is tender and the beef is well browned (about 8-10 minutes).
5. Season with salt and pepper. Drain any excess grease.
6. Add the pasta sauce and water, and mix well.

Transfer the meat mixture to a bowl and let the electric pressure cooker cool down (press cancel, or unplug it).

<u>To assemble and cook</u>

7. Make sure the pot has cooled down.
8. Pour ¼ inch of water into the pot.
9. Scoop about a fifth of the meat mixture into the pot and spread it out evenly.
10. Follow with a layer of noodles.
11. Use about a third of the cheese mixture to make the next layer.
12. Follow this cheese layer with another layer of the meat mixture and then with noodles.
13. Repeat the layering. You should end with noodles topped with the meat mixture. You should have one portion of grated mozzarella left.
14. Close the lid and lock it. Set the timer to 7 minutes.

15. When the cooking time is complete, use quick release.
16. Open the pot and sprinkle mozzarella on top.
17. Cover it again, and let it sit for 10 minutes (if it seems watery, leave it a little longer).

Nutrition (per serving)
Calories 455, carbs 33 g, fat 23g, protein 25 g, sodium 297 mg

Mexican Green Rice

Serves 3
Preparation time: 5 minutes
Cooking time: 3 minutes

Ingredients
1 ¼ cups chicken stock
1 cup uncooked long grain rice

For green sauce
½ cup avocado
½ cup fresh cilantro
¼ cup green salsa
Salt and pepper

Directions

1. Combine the green sauce ingredients in a blender, and process them. The consistency should be similar to sour cream. Add a little water, if needed. Set it aside.
2. Place the rice and stock into the electric pressure cooker's pot, stirring a little.
3. Cover and lock the lid, and set the timer to 3 minutes.
4. Allow natural release for 10 minutes, and then use quick release.
5. Fluff the rice and let it sit for 5-10 minutes.
6. Add the green sauce to the rice, mixing thoroughly.
7. Adjust the taste with more salt and pepper, if needed.
8. Serve.

Nutrition (per serving)
Calories 26, carbs 48 g, fat 5 g, protein 6 g, sodium 473 mg

Risotto with Zucchini

Serves 6
Preparation time: 5 minutes
Cooking time: 15 minutes

Ingredients

2-3 tablespoons olive oil
1 onion, chopped
1 zucchini, diced, divided
2 cups Arborio rice
2 tablespoons white wine
4 cups vegetable broth
1 tablespoon butter
1 tablespoon Parmesan cheese
Salt and pepper, to taste

Directions

1. Set the electric pressure cooker to sauté.
2. When it is hot enough, add the onion and ¼ cup of the zucchini, and cook until the onion is translucent (about 5 minutes).
3. Add the rice, stirring continuously, until it is toasted (you see it begin to turn golden in color).
4. Add the wine, and loosen any bits stuck to the bottom of the pan.
5. Keep stirring until the wine dries up.
6. Stir in the broth, together with the rest of the zucchini, and quickly close the pot to prevent further evaporation.
7. Set the timer to 6 minutes.
8. When the cooking time is done, use quick release.
9. Switch off or unplug the electric pressure cooker, open it, and carefully remove the inner pot.

10. Place the insert on a rack and stir the rice to help it absorb the excess moisture (about 1 minute). If the rice is still too wet, return it to the cooker's pot, set it to sauté, and stir continuously until you get the right consistency.
11. Stir in the butter and Parmesan.
12. Season with salt and pepper.

Nutrition (per serving)
Calories 270, carbs 50 g, fat 4.1 g, protein 7 g, sodium 760 mg

Spaghetti with Meatballs

Serves 4
Preparation time: 15 minutes
Cooking time: 19 minutes

Ingredients
1 pound spaghetti noodles
Parmesan, grated, for topping

For the meatballs
1 pound ground beef
½ cup bread crumbs
¼ cup milk
½ cup parsley, chopped
½ cup Parmesan cheese, grated
1 egg, slightly beaten
½ teaspoon salt
½ teaspoon pepper
1 clove garlic, minced

For the spaghetti sauce
1 tablespoon olive oil
1 small onion, minced
3 cloves garlic, peeled and minced
1 tablespoon tomato paste
1 teaspoon dried basil
1 teaspoon oregano
½ teaspoon salt
½ teaspoon black pepper
½ cup red wine or beef broth2 (28 ounce) cans tomato sauce
2 bay leaves

Directions

1. Cook the spaghetti according to the packaging instructions. Set it aside, and cover it to keep it moist.

For the spaghetti sauce

2. Set the electric pressure cooker to sauté and wait until it is hot.
3. Add the oil and sauté the onion until it is softened (about 3 minutes).
4. Stir in the garlic and cook until it is fragrant (about 1 minute).
5. Add the tomato paste, basil, oregano, salt, and pepper. Stir continuously, until the onions acquire the color of the paste (about 2 minutes).
6. Add the broth or wine, loosening any bits from the bottom of the pan.
7. Pour in the tomato sauce, and add the bay leaves.
8. Leave the lid open and let the sauce simmer (about 5 minutes).

For the meatballs

9. Prepare the meatballs while the sauce is simmering.
10. Put the breadcrumbs in a bowl and add the milk. Let it sit to allow the breadcrumbs to absorb the milk (about 1 minute).
11. Add the rest of the ingredients, and mix well.
12. Using a small ice cream scoop or a tablespoon, shape the mixture into balls and drop them into the sauce.
13. Close and lock the lid, and set the timer to 8 minutes.
14. When the pressure cooking is done, use natural release for 10 minutes, and then quick release.

15.	If the sauce still needs to be thickened, set the electric pressure cooker to sauté, and cook until the sauce is the right consistency (about 10 minutes). Discard the bay leaves.
16.	Serve the sauce and meatballs over cooked the spaghetti, sprinkled with grated Parmesan.

Nutrition (per serving)
Calories 676, carbs 87 g, fat 22 g, protein 34 g, sodium 1973 mg

Vegetarian Recipes

Mashed Potatoes

Serves 2-4
Preparation time: 10 minutes
Cooking time: 10 minutes

Ingredients
4 russet potatoes, peeled and quartered
2 tablespoons unsalted butter
2 cloves garlic, minced
Pinch of salt
½ cup milk
2 tablespoons Parmesan cheese, grated
Salt and black pepper, to taste

Directions

1. Fill an electric pressure cooker's pot with 1 cup of water.
2. Place the potatoes in the steaming basket.
3. Put the trivet in the pot and position the steaming basket over it.
4. Close and lock the lid. Set the manual timer to 8 minutes.
5. After cooking, use quick release.
6. While the potatoes are cooking, prepare the milk mixture.
7. Melt the butter in a saucepan over medium heat.
8. Add the garlic and salt, cooking until the garlic is golden brown (about 2 minutes).
9. Stir in the milk, loosening any bits stuck to the bottom of the pan.
10. Remove the pot from the heat and set it aside.
11. Transfer the potatoes to a large bowl, and use a potato masher to mash them.

12. Pour in half of the milk mixture and continue mashing to incorporate.
13. Gradually add the remaining milk mixture until the desired texture is attained.
14. Add the Parmesan cheese and season with salt and pepper.
15. Serve while warm.

Nutrition (per serving)
Calories 224, carbs 35 g, fat 7 g, protein 6 g, sodium 130 mg

Refried Beans

Serves 10-12
Preparation time: 5 minutes
Cooking time: 28 minutes

Ingredients
2 cups dried pinto beans, rinsed well, drained (do not soak)
1 large onion, quartered
4 cloves of garlic, peeled and roughly chopped
1 teaspoon salt
1 teaspoon paprika
1 teaspoon chili powder
1 teaspoon cumin
½ teaspoon black pepper
½ cup salsa
1 cup of vegetable stock
2 cups water

Directions

1. Put all the ingredients in an electric pressure cooker.
2. Close and lock the lid. Set the timer to 28 minutes.
3. When the cooking cycle is done, use natural release for 10 minutes, and then quick release or simply wait for the pot to be fully depressurized before opening it.
4. Use a potato masher or blender to get the consistency you want – the beans can be chunky, creamy, or thin. For thicker consistency, scoop or drain some of the liquid before mashing. The liquid can be added back gradually to adjust the texture.

Nutrition (per serving)
Calories 312, carbs 61 g, fat 2 g, protein 16 g, sodium 2168 mg

Sicilian Vegetable Medley

Serves 4
Preparation time: 10 minutes plus 30 minutes waiting time
Cooking time: 10 minutes

Ingredients
1 large eggplant, cubed (1-inch pieces)
1 teaspoon salt
¼ cup olive oil
2 medium potatoes, cubed (¾-inch pieces)
1 medium bell pepper, cut into large strips
1 onion, sliced
2 medium zucchini, cut into rounds (about ¼-inch thick)
1 tablespoon capers, strained and rinsed
1 tablespoons raisins, re-hydrated and drained
¼ cup olives, pitted
2 tablespoons pine nuts, divided
1 bunch basil, chopped, divided
Salt and pepper, to taste
10 cherry tomatoes, halved

For the dressing
⅓ cup olive oil
2 tablespoons balsamic vinegar
1 teaspoon honey or brown sugar, or to taste
Dash of salt
Dash of pepper

Directions

1. Whisk together the ingredients for the dressing. Set it aside.
2. Place the eggplant cubes in a colander over a bowl and sprinkle them with salt. Leave them to sit for 30 minutes to an hour. You may put a weight over the eggplant to help squeeze out bitter-tasting moisture. Wipe it off with paper towels.
3. Set the electric pressure cooker to sauté.
4. When the pot is hot, add the olive oil.
5. Begin by adding the eggplant and potato, stirring continuously (about 3 minutes).
6. Next, add the peppers and onion (2 minutes).
7. Follow with zucchini (2 minutes).
8. Gently stir in the capers, raisins, olives, half of the pine nuts, half of the basil, and salt and pepper.
9. Close and lock the lid.
10. Set the timer to 3 minutes.
11. When the time is up, depressurize using quick release.
12. Immediately transfer the vegetables to a serving dish to prevent overcooking.
13. Let them cool to room temperature.
14. Add the tomatoes and remaining pine nuts, as well as the basil.
15. Drizzle with the dressing.

Nutrition (per serving)
Calories 368, carbs 36 g, fat 24 g, protein 4 g, sodium 1246 mg

Steamed Artichoke Blooms

Serves 3
Preparation time: 15 minutes
Cooking time: 20 minutes

Ingredients
3 artichokes, scrubbed (to remove bitter film), topped and tailed, de-thorned
1 lemon, halved
6 cloves garlic, minced
2 bay leaves

Directions

1. Squeeze half the lemon over the artichokes and rub the juice in to prevent browning. Save and slice the squished peel.
2. Thinly slice the rest of the lemon.
3. Pour 2 cups of water into the cooker's pot and add the lemon slices (including the squished peel), together with the garlic and bay leaves.
4. Place the trivet into the pot. Put the artichokes, stem side up, on it.
5. Close and lock the lid, and set the timer to 20 minutes.
6. After cooking, use quick release.
7. Test for doneness by inserting a knife through the artichoke, it should glide in easily.
8. Transfer the artichokes to a tray and cut them in half, lengthwise.
9. Scoop out the purple centers with a spoon, and discard them.
10. Serve with melted butter, vinaigrette, or mayonnaise.

Nutrition (per serving)
Calories 76, carbs 17 g, fat 0 g, protein 5 g, sodium 152 mg

Brussels Sprouts with Sweet Orange Sauce

Serves 8
Preparation time: 10 minutes
Cooking time: 3 minutes

Ingredients

1 ½ pounds Brussels sprouts, de-stemmed, and rinsed
¼ cup freshly squeezed orange juice
1 teaspoon orange zest, grated
1 tablespoon butter
2 tablespoons maple syrup
Salt and pepper, to taste

Directions

1. Keep the Brussels sprouts uniform in size by cutting large pieces in half, if necessary.
2. Place all the ingredients in the electric pressure cooker.
3. Close and lock the lid, and set the timer to 3 minutes.
4. After cooking, use quick release.
5. The sprouts should be easy to pierce with a fork. You may increase or decrease the cooking time, depending on the texture you prefer.
6. Stir, and transfer them to a serving dish. Make sure each piece is coated with sauce.
7. Serve warm.

Nutrition (per serving)

Calories 65, carbs 12 g, fat 2 g, protein 3 g, sodium 179 mg

Dessert Recipes

Baked Apples

Serves 6
Preparation time: 5 minutes
Cooking time: 10 minutes

Ingredients
6 apples
½ cup unsweetened apple juice
½ cup red wine
¼ cup raisins
1 teaspoon cinnamon powder
¼ cup brown sugar, packed

Directions

1. Arrange the apples in the bottom of the pressure cooker.
2. Pour in the apple juice and red wine.
3. Sprinkle with raisins, cinnamon, and sugar.
4. Close and lock the lid.
5. Set the timer to 10 minutes.
6. Switch off or unplug the electric pressure cooker, and allow natural release.
7. Spoon sauce over the apples, and serve.

Nutrition (per serving)
Calories 203 g, carbs 52 g, fat 1 g, protein 1 g, sodium 7 mg

Cheese Flan

Serves 8
Preparation time: 15 minutes
Cooking time: 15 minutes

Ingredients
1 (8 ounce) package cream cheese, softened
5 eggs
1 (14 ounce) can sweetened condensed milk
1 (12 ounce) can evaporated milk
1 teaspoon vanilla
Dash cinnamon
Dash nutmeg

For the caramel
½ cup sugar

Directions
To make the caramel

1. Prepare a flan pan, or one that will fit inside your cooker's pot.
2. Place the ½ cup of sugar in a saucepan.
3. Heat over medium heat. DO NOT STIR. Simply allow the sugar to melt and come to a boil. At this point, you can lift the pot and swirl the mixture gently. Watch carefully, because it can burn in a matter of seconds.
4. When you notice some browning, swirl again. The caramel is done when the whole mixture is amber brown.
5. Pour the caramel into the flan pan. Swirl to spread it evenly over the bottom. Set It aside.

To make the flan

6. Cream the cheese in a bowl with a mixer.
7. Add the eggs one at a time, mixing after each addition.
8. Add the rest of the ingredients, and mix to combine.
9. Pour the filling into the flan pan.
10. Pour water into the cooker's pot until it is 2 inches deep.
11. Put in the trivet and place the flan on top.
12. Cover and lock the lid, and set the timer to 15 minutes.
13. Switch off or unplug the electric pressure cooker and allow natural release.
14. Remove the flan pan from the pot and let it cool to room temperature.
15. Refrigerate for at least 6 hours.
16. Loosen the edges using a knife, and flip the flan over a serving plate. The plate should be somewhat larger that the flan, to catch the dripping caramel at the sides.

Nutrition (per serving)
Calories 350, carbs 35 g, fat 19 g, protein 12 g, sodium 213 mg

Crème Brulée

Serves 6
Preparation time: 20 minutes
Cooking time: 6 minutes

Ingredients
8 egg yolks
⅓ cup granulated sugar
Pinch salt
2 cups heavy cream
1 ½ teaspoons vanilla
6 tablespoons superfine sugar, for caramelized topping

Directions

1. Whisk the egg yolks, granulated sugar, and salt in a large bowl until well blended.
2. Add the cream and vanilla, whisking well.
3. Strain the mixture into a container with a spout.
4. Pour the filling into 6 custard cups or ramekins. Cover each container snugly with foil.
5. Place a trivet or steaming basket into the electric pressure cooker's pot and pour in 1 ½ cups of water.
6. Arrange the cups on the trivet or steaming basket. You can stack them pyramid-style, or place a second trivet on top.
7. Close and lock the lid, and set the timer to 6 minutes.
8. Natural release for 10 minutes and then quick release.
9. Remove the cups and let them cool on a rack. Replace the foil with plastic wrap.
10. Refrigerate from overnight to 48 hours.
11. Sprinkle 1 tablespoon of superfine sugar over the surface of one cup of custard.

12. Hold a kitchen torch 2 inches away, and caramelize the sugar in a circling motion. Do the same to the rest of the cups. You may also place the sprinkled cups on the highest shelf in a broiler at high heat. Watch carefully and turn the cups for even browning (about 10 minutes).

Nutrition (per serving)
Calories 400, carbs 23 g, fat 30 g, protein 4 g, sodium 37 mg

Key Lime Pie

Serves 6-8
Preparation time: 30 minutes
Cooking time: 15 minutes

Ingredients

For the graham cracker crust
¾ cup graham cracker crumbs (about 5-10 crackers)
3 tablespoons unsalted butter, melted
1 tablespoon sugar

For the filling
4 large egg yolks
1 (14 ounce) can sweetened condensed milk
½ cup fresh key lime juice (or combination of lemon and lime juice)
⅓ cup sour cream
2 tablespoons grated lime zest

Directions

1. Prepare a springform pan with cooking spray.

To make the crust

2. Mix the crust ingredients together and press them down evenly into the bottom of the springform pan.
3. Freeze for at least 10 minutes.

To make the filling

4. Use a mixer to beat the egg yolks until they are light and lemony in color.
5. Add the condensed milk and mix until thickened.
6. Gradually add the lime juice while mixing, until smooth.
7. Stir in the sour cream and zest.
8. Pour the mixture into the pan, and cover with aluminum foil.
9. Pour 1 cup of water into the cooker's pot. Place the trivet inside.
10. Using a foil sling, lower the pan into the pressure cooker's pot.
11. Close and lock the lid, and set the timer to 15 minutes.
12. When the cooking cycle is done, allow natural release for 10 minutes, and then use quick release.
13. Slide a knife into the center of the pie to check for doneness. It should slide out clean. If center is not yet done, cook 5 minutes more.
14. Remove the foil and cool the pie on a rack.
15. Cover with plastic wrap and refrigerate for at least 4 hours before serving.

Nutrition (per serving)
Calories 255, carbs 3 g, fat 12 g, protein 7 g, sodium 118 mg

Printed in Great Britain
by Amazon